This book belongs to

A is for apple

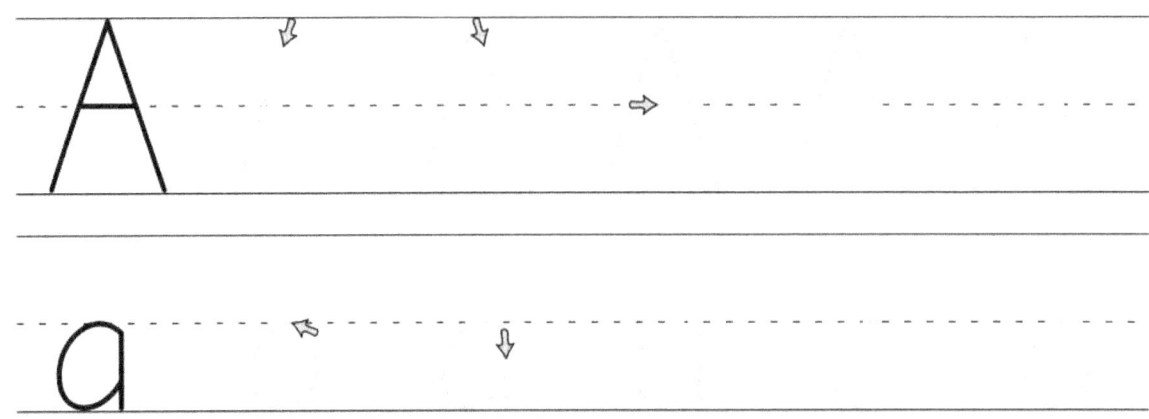

B is for bear

B

b

C is for cat

C

C

D is for dog

E is for elephant

E

e

F is for fish

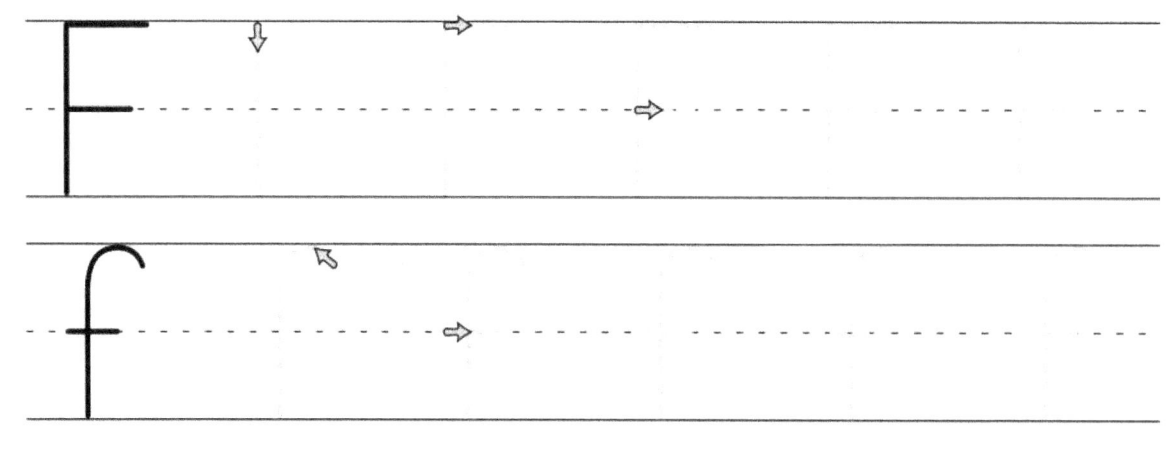

G is for giraffe

H is for hippo

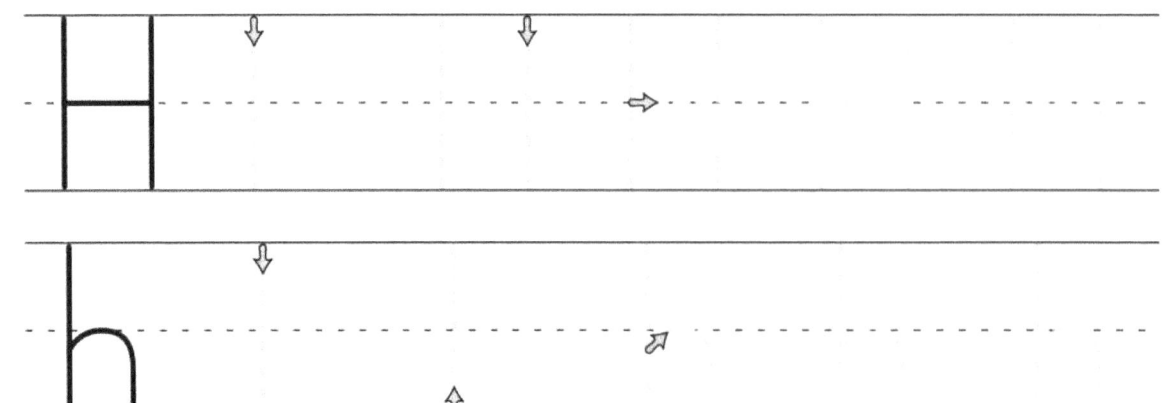

I is for iguana

J is for jaguar

K is for koala

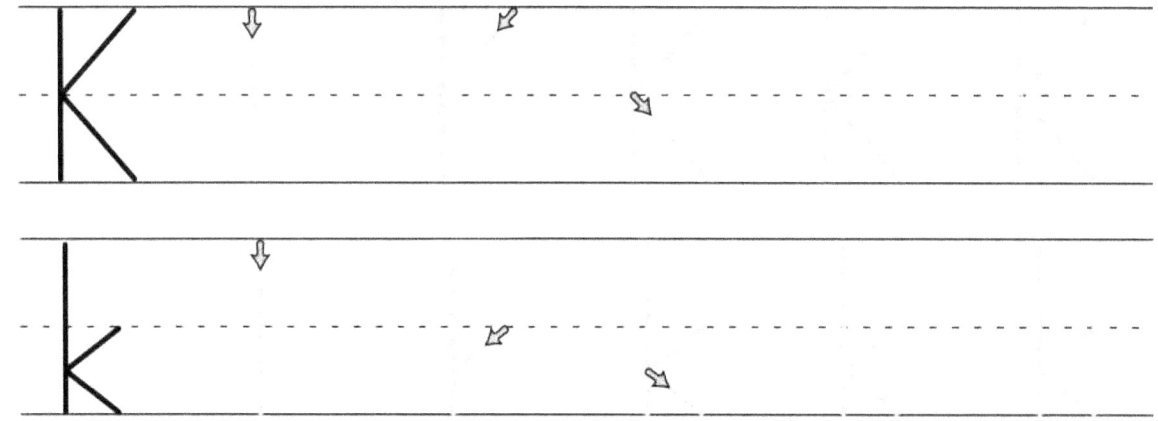

L is for lion

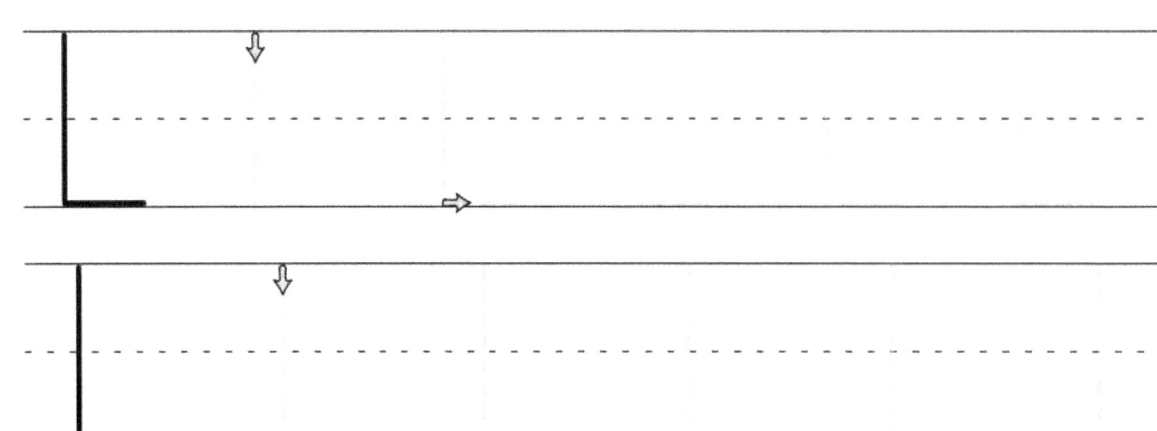

M is for monkey

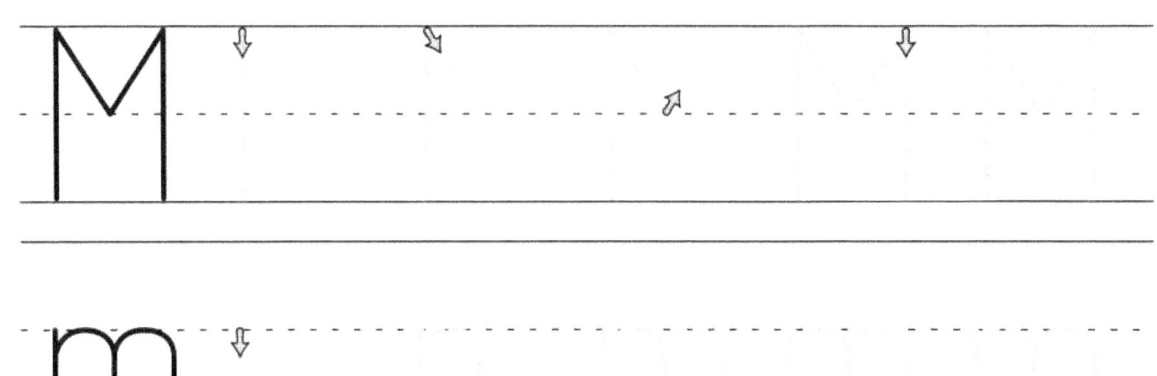

N is for narwhal

N

n

P is for panda

P

P

Q is for quail

R is for rabbit

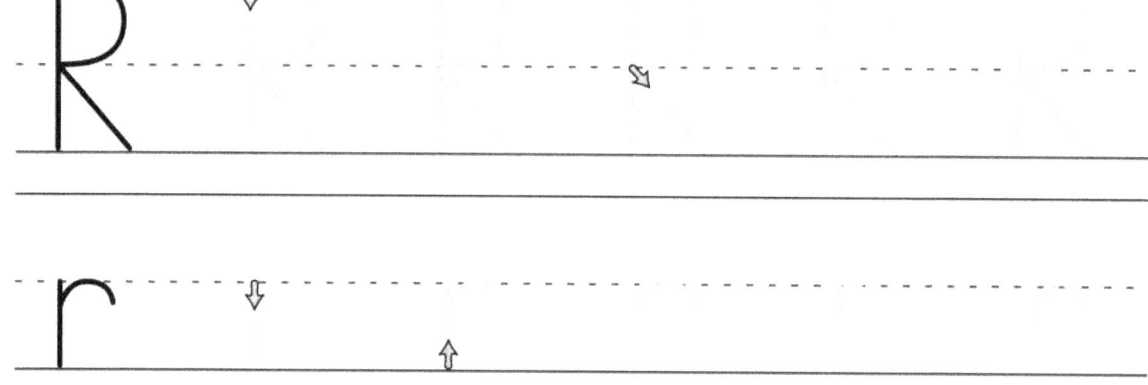

S is for sheep

S

s

T is for tiger

U is for unicorn

U

U

V is for vulture

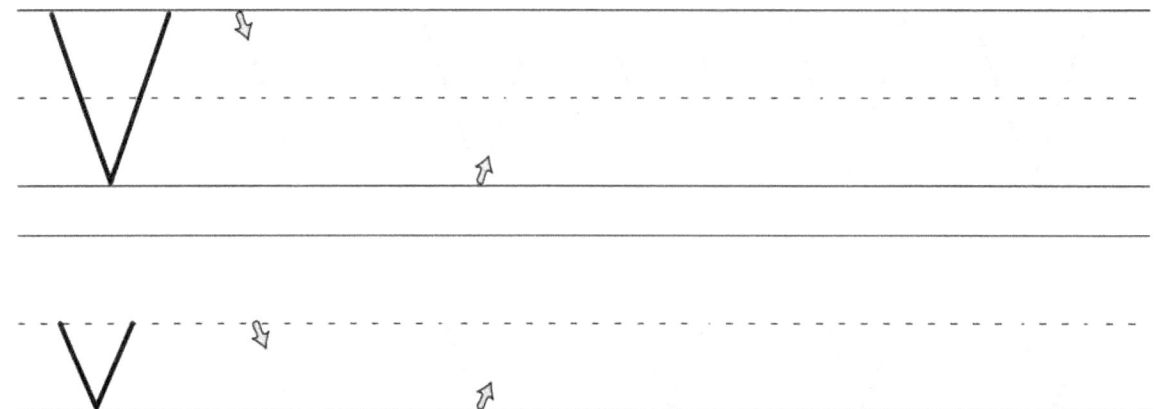

W is for wolf

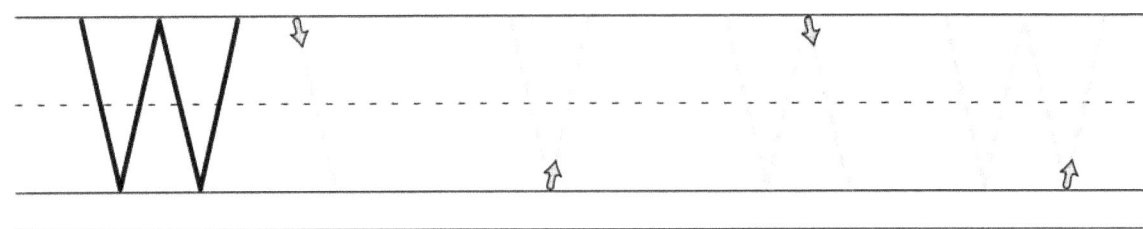

X is for X-ray fish

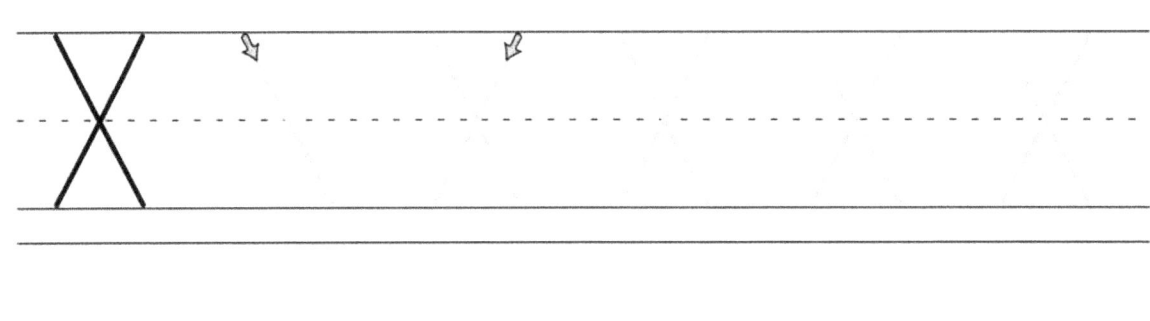

Y is for yak

Z is for zebra

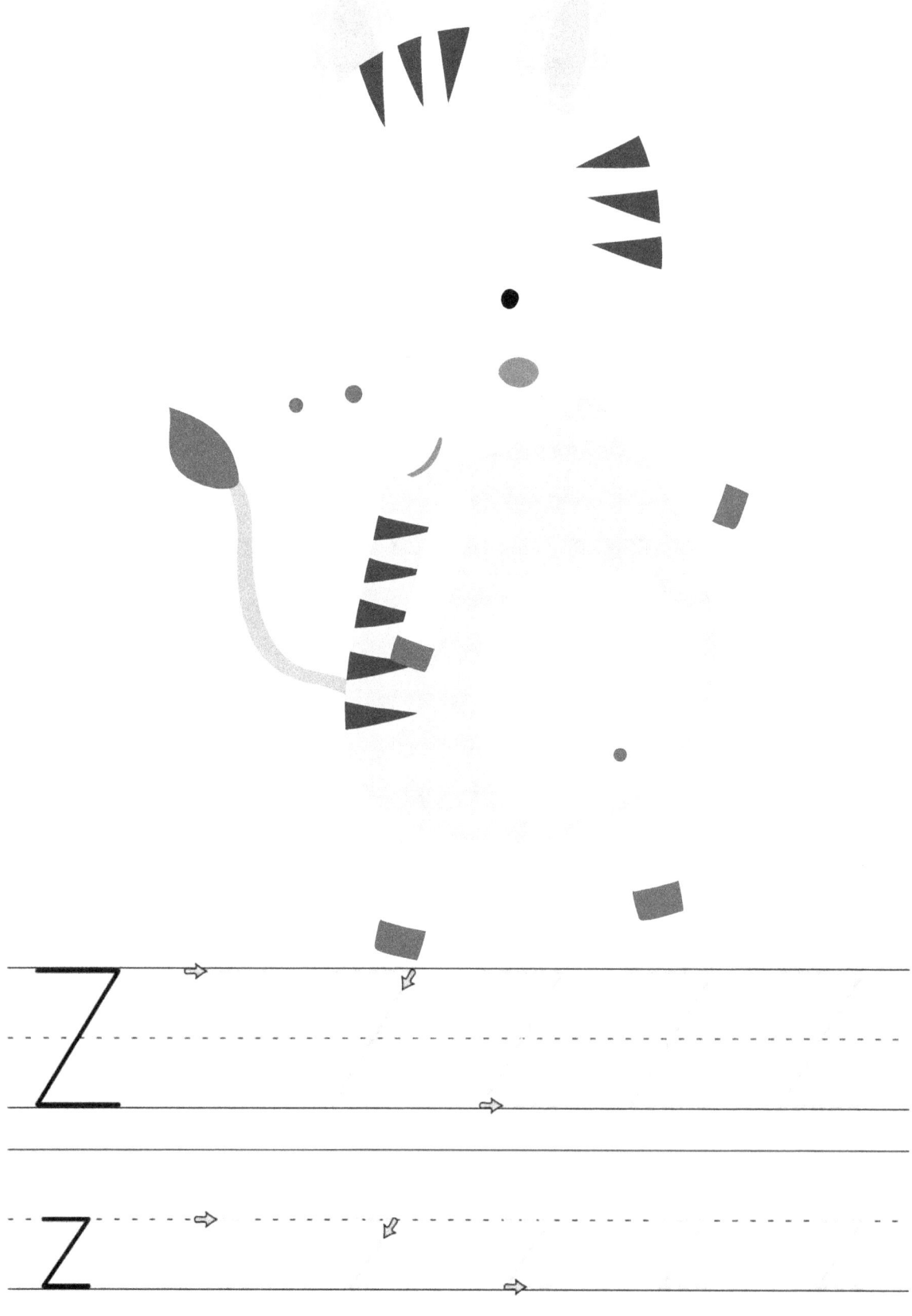